A HANDBOOK
for
MIGRANT YOUTH

PEER TO PEER WISDOM FROM THOSE
WHO'VE BEEN THERE, DONE THAT

LiME Youth
Compiled by Ephraim Osaghae

Copyright @2019 by Migrants Professional Bridge Incorporated

Publishing Support: Achievers World

Disclaimer: The information provided within this publication, including observations made and lessons learned, are of the nature of general comments only. While we try to keep the information up-to-date and correct, there are no representations or warranties, express or implied, about the completeness, accuracy, reliability, suitability or availability with respect to the information, products, services or related graphics contained in this publication for any purpose. Any use of this information is at your own risk. It is recommended that readers obtain their own independent information and advice, where applicable.

All rights reserved. No part of this publication may be reproduced, distributed or transmitted in any form or by any means, including photocopying, recording or other electronic or mechanical methods, without the prior written permission of Migrants Professional Bridge Incorporated.

ISBN (Paperback): 978-0-6484799-1-8
ISBN (eBook): 978-0-6484799-2-5

Dedication

To LiME Parents:

Neil & Lea Menezes, Louis & Omoye Okiwelu, Nestor & Agness Ngandu, Martin & Yuni Liem, Ebun Enilari, Martin & Amy Deng, Marlon & Bonny Wilson, Ephraim & Esosa Osaghae, Femi & Oludotun Oyewopo, Lakers & Morenikeji Komaiya, Frederick & Joy Idehen, Emmanuel & Victoria Shyllon, Marco Issaya & Leocadia Niyonkuru, Sipho & Thobile Mazibuko, James & Beena Samuel, Fred Chansongo, Richard & Elizabeth Amudo, Lawrence & Nwakego Anwasi, and Mary Zowonu

Acknowledgement

The LiME support network is broad and almost endless. The Board of Migrants' Professional Bridge Incorporated would like to commend our LiME Youth Group for their courage and determination. They believe in themselves, the LiME vision and the deeper urge to influence their generation for good. This book is one of the early results. You guys rock!

Secondly, we would like to thank our LiME Coordinators, Facilitators, Mentors and Special Guests. They include Ephraim Osaghae, Femi Oyewopo, Samuel Shyllon, Richard Amudo, John & Brenda Palmer, Emma Kake, Liam Palmer, Lakers Komaiya, Rohit & Lakshmi Kanchi, Gabriel Adesanya, Esther Mwathi, Cornelius Itotoh, Natasha Van Wyk, Mireille Toulekima, Caroline Surtees, Kim Charles, Gladys Serugga Miss Africa Perth (2018) and many more; they're too numerous to mention here. Many went beyond the usual call for support to ensure the smooth running of the LiME initiative.

Finally, we acknowledge LiME Sponsors (cash and kind). They include City of Gosnells, City of Canning, Perth Airport, Department of Communities, Relationship Australia WA, BHP, Afropacific Media, Business Station, Cr Glenn Dewhurst, Cr Paul Ng and Hon Bill Johnston MLA.

Preface

This handbook is primarily aimed at providing support and soft landing for new and emerging migrant youth in Australia. However, the information is globally relevant.

LiME was envisioned, conceptualized and implemented on the premise that migrant youth do have a lot to offer to the country that have embraced them and given them the opportunity and enabling environment to flourish. While undertaking capacity-building activities on a fortnightly basis over the 3 phases of the LiME project, the aim was always to unleash greatness in the participating youth (LiMErs) who will then become catalysts for further positive changes in the wider community and for generations of young people.

This book is a bit of evidence that the process of unleashing this greatness has begun. The seed has been sown. The germination has commenced. The LiME tree is spreading already. Hopefully, so many in our current and upcoming generations will take cover under its branches, many will receive healings from its contents and many more will eat its life-giving fruits.

Ephraim Osaghae, Founder and COO of Migrants' Professional Bridge Incorporated, creator, lead facilitator and Project Leader for LiME

Table of Contents

1.0 LiME – Leadership in Motion & Experience 1

    1.1 LiME Pilot: Feb – Aug 2018 3

    1.2 LiME 2.0: Aug – Dec 2018 11

    1.3 LiME 3.0: Feb – Jun 2019 12

2.0 A Quick Introduction to Australia, its Multiculturalism and Opportunities 17

    2.1 A Brief History and Facts About Australia 18

    2.2 Acknowledgement & Welcome to Country and Why It Is Important ... 19

    2.3 Multicultural Australia 20

    2.4 Opportunities for Youth in Australia 27

3.0 Education Pathways 31

    3.1 Levels of Education in Australia 33

    3.2 Some Important Aspects of K-12 Education in Western Australia 35

4.0 Youth & Technology 41

    4.1 Technology for Schools and Learning 43

    4.2 Technology for Play, Entertainment and Everyday Living 43

    4.3 Technology for Work and Business 44

    4.4 Technology for the Future 45

    4.5 Youth and Technology: The Balance 46

5.0 Internet, Social Media and Gaming 49
5.1 Why Internet, Social Media and Gaming? 50
5.2 Different Types of Social Media and Gaming 52
5.3 Advantages and Disadvantages of Internet, Social Media and Gaming 58
5.4 Striking the Right Balance 62

6.0 Youth & Finances 65
6.1 Introduction to Financial Education 65
6.2 Saving Money 67
6.3 Starting a Money-Saving Habit 67
6.4 The Fear of Missing Out 68
6.5 Become Independent and Entrepreneurial 68
6.6 Get Educated! 69

7.0 Youth and mental Health 73
7.1 Mental Health 75
7.2 Mental Illness 76
7.3 Youth and Mental Illnesses 77
7.4 Achieving and Staying Mentally Healthy 78

8.0 Concluding Remarks 83

1.0 LiME – Leadership in Motion & Experience

Maria Shyllon

The LiME Project had its first meeting on the 23rd of February, 2018. From then on, every Saturday, the members of the project would come together to immerse themselves into the content that LiME provided for them. The members consisted of people of ages 12 – 17 years, referred to as LiMErs. Although, throughout the duration of the LiME project, the group was also joined by some eager and enthusiastic primary school kids of 10-11 years of age.

LiME was to be a place of multiculturalism, diversity and inclusion. A place where young people could come and learn skills, together with fellow young people, that would help them in their future careers. These skills included the art of communication, teamwork and cooperation, self-discovery and goal setting. LiMErs also had access to a number of mentors from multiple disciplines to gain inspirations and insights from their experiences. There were also regular time-slots available for play and games.

A Handbook for Migrant Youth

LiME in Session

LiME – Leadership in Motion & Experience

1.1 LiME Pilot: Feb – Aug 2018

During the first phase of LiME, we had the Toastmasters Gavel Club, which was conducted during our regular meetings. This part of LiME, at least for me, was the most beneficial. We would prepare speeches to present to our peers and get evaluated for our presenting skills. With that, we learnt various skills such as how to stand on stage, voice projection, making use of notes and other invaluable ones lessons.

LiME Gavel – Communication and Leadership Sessions

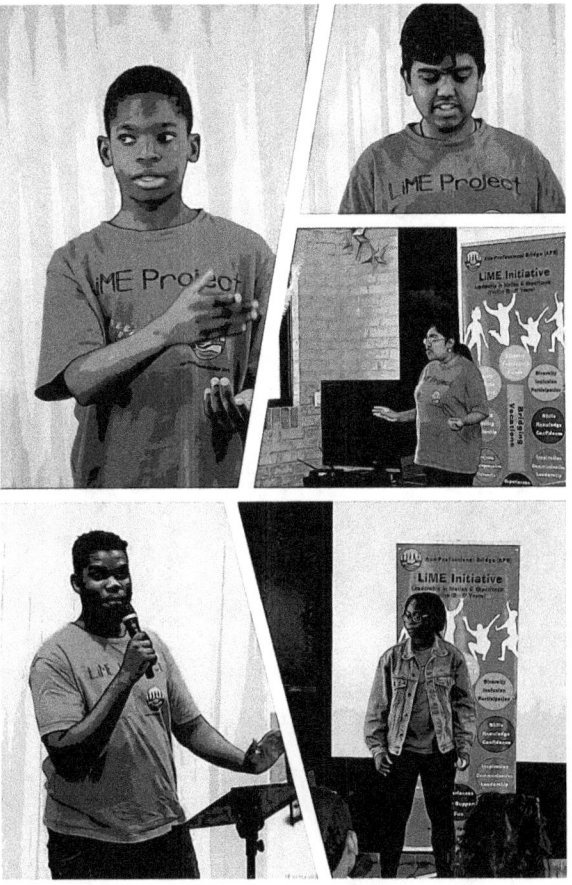

A Handbook for Migrant Youth

We LiMErs learnt a lot from our mentors about time management and goal setting, defining for ourselves our identities and some principles of handling money. Occasionally, we had talks from specific groups of people. We have had people come talk to us about evolving technologies (like Artificial Intelligence (AI) and machine learning), entrepreneurship, etc.

LiME in Session – with Coordinators, Mentors & Facilitators

A Handbook for Migrant Youth

LiME – Leadership in Motion & Experience

Throughout the year, LiMErs partook in several excursions, one of which was a trip to the BHP in Perth. The members were able get insights into the various job roles available in the company and what their responsibilities would be. It was a valuable experience for all LiMErs, particularly those who were interested in mining and other areas within BHP's line of work.

LiMErs BHP Trip

During the third quarter, LiMErs and their parents had a day camp where discussions were held about education pathways, communication within the family and lots of fun games and play. The highlight of the camp was the family session when LiMErs and their parents were divided into two separate groups and there were discussions about ways of expressing ourselves and talking about aspects of our own personalities.

LiMErs Camp

This phase of LiME ended with a well-earned and enjoyable Award Ceremony where we had LiME Sponsors, Mayor of City of Canning and Mayor of City of Gosnells in attendance. Remarkably, the whole event was run by LiME youth – the MC, couple of speeches, etc.

LiME Awards

LiME – Leadership in Motion & Experience

1.2 LiME 2.0: Aug – Dec 2018

During the second phase of LiME, LiME 2.0, there was a greater focus on entrepreneurship. Here, we created the 'LiME Tank' as a part of our activities. The LiME tank consisted of brainstorming sessions to come up with business related and other innovative ideas. It also involved working in groups and developing team skills.

LiME Tank Entrepreneurship Sessions

1.3 LiME 3.0: Feb – Jun 2019

LiME 3.0 also involved a LiME Think Tank wherein we held regular brainstorming sessions for looking into solutions to pertinent social issues relating to young people in our age bracket. It quickly evolved to a LiME book project (this book): A Handbook for Migrant Youth.

With support from our coaches and mentors and a publisher, the LiME Youth group has worked together in teams to develop and contribute articles on relevant topics. The book is aimed at providing peer to peer wisdom from LiMErs who've been there, done that.

LiME Think Tank / Book Project in Session

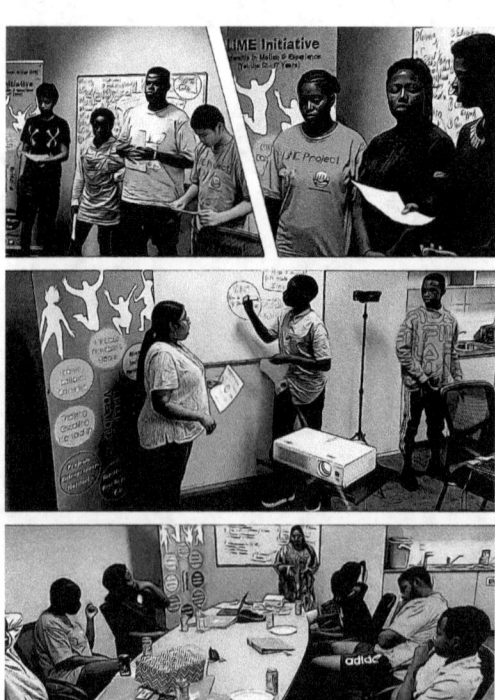

New and emerging teenagers of migrant backgrounds will find this book particularly useful.

Often, lots of support and guidance is available for parents and adults as they become residents of a new country. However, less attention is given to younger migrants. This gap can create detrimental consequences for the youth including social isolation, loss of direction and focus, feeling unsupported and uprooted, helplessness, frustration and irritation due to changes in circumstances, experiencing identity crises, etc.

All young people, migrants as well as those who are already established in the new country will find information in this book very useful. And they can be use it to inspire them.

Parents, mentors, teachers and school administrators will find valuable tips and suggestions in this book that will help them in their ongoing efforts to make great leaders of their children, mentees and students.

The content in this book will also provide government office holders, policy makers and service providers with real stories and lived experiences from young people themselves.

Finally, while Australia is the context for this book, the principles and lessons are applicable across the globe.

> *The skills I learnt at LiME, have given me the courage and confidence to do things I never thought I could do, like speaking in front of a big crowd and being a leader.*

Being a part of the LiME group was a great experience that helped me to grow as a person. Going every week, I was able to interact with diverse and creative individuals and I was able to learn from them all. I also made some great friends at the same time.

At LiME, I was able to learn skills that helped me to grow in my confidence. The skills I learnt have given me the courage and confidence to do things I never thought I could do, like speaking in front of a big crowd and being a leader.

Reflection 1.0:

- Why are youth groups like LiME important to our communities and nation? Why is it important for every youth to belong to one? Such groups could be based in schools, workplaces or communities. Write down a few lines to capture your reflections.

  _____
  _____
  _____

- Who are your friends? How kind and friendly are you? Do you help your friends to have fun and be successful in their endeavours despite the challenges of life? Do they do the same for you? Write down a few thoughts and discuss with a mentor where possible.

  _____
  _____
  _____

- Do you have mentors? If yes, list a few of them. Do you respect and listen to them as they provide you with valuable guidance? Family members, school teachers, community leaders could be mentors. If you don't have mentors, why?

  _____
  _____
  _____

2.0 A Quick Introduction to Australia, its Multiculturalism and Opportunities

Niche Deng, Esther Batty, Solotin Santana, Gracia Ngandu, Abraham Oyewopo, Joy Ngandu and Fatiha Enilari

Australia has a rich multicultural history, including the thousands of migrants who have settled here over the years. Indeed, the country's development and growth is are very much associated with this migrant population as well as the opportunities that are provided for people who come from around the world to reside and raise families and generations in the country.

2.1 A Brief History and Facts About Australia

Australia is located in the continent of Oceania and it's between the South Pacific and Indian Ocean. Australia holds the world's largest coral reef known as the Great Barrier Reef, located on the north east side of Australia, off the coast of Queensland. Canberra is the capital city and with a population is of roughly about 25 million as at 2019.

Australia's indigenous people have lived in the nation for a very long time. There were roughly 300,000 and 1 million Aborigines living in the country before the colonists arrived. Dutch were the first to sight Australia back in 1606, much before the arrival of Captain Cook in 1770. New South Wales was established as a penal colony in 1788. This continued till 1848 (www.insiderguides.com.au).

In 1901, Australia became an independent nation and the commonwealth was created. Canberra was designated to be our capital during this time.

In April 1915, the Australian and New Zealand Army Corps (ANZACs) took part in World War I (WWI), at Gallipoli. Almost 39% of Australia's male population between the ages of 18 and 44

> *ANZAC: to honour, to respect, to celebrate, and to remember the soldiers that fought for Australia and New Zealand in the Gallipoli and Peninsula war.*

had enlisted to fight this war (as enlisting was compulsory unless one was ill). Though we were defeated, the battle is of great significance today. April 25th, the day on which we landed on Gallipoli, is known as ANZAC Day, an annual national public holiday in which all Australians pay their respects to those who sacrifice their lives for our country, both past and present.

Australia has people belonging to diverse religious groups. In 2016, the Australian census found that the dominant religion was Christianity with 12 million people or 86% of the population belonging to this group (Australian Bureau of Statistics – www.abs.gov.au).

The other prominent religions are:

- Islam (600,000 people)
- Buddhism (560,000)
- Hinduism (440,000)
- Sikhism (130,000)
- Judaism (90,000)

Australia remains a predominately religious country. And, roughly 30% of Australians consider themselves non-religious or atheists. (Australian Bureau of Statistics – www.abs.gov.au)

2.2 Acknowledgement & Welcome to Country and Why It Is Important

Acknowledgement to Country is a way of recognising the aboriginal culture and history. This is usually performed at as a ceremony. The ceremony can be conducted by an indigenous or non-indigenous person, to pay respect to the fact that we are standing and living on what is aboriginal land. However, the person playing the role must ensure that they pronounce the words correctly, as wrong pronunciations could offend the Aboriginal people (www.commonground.org.au).

Welcome to country is conducted by a traditional owner of the land belonging to the local region where the event is being held. It is commonly performed by delivering speeches in the relevant language and/or by means of performing traditional dances.

These traditional rites are important because Aboriginal and Torres Strait Islander people have experienced significant exclusion from the Australian society for many years.

> *We must continue to acknowledge the first people of our nation and validate the true history of the land that we all now call home*

Furthermore, many non-indigenous people get the opportunity to learn about these native cultures this way.

2.3 Multicultural Australia

Australia is a multicultural country that is culturally diverse in people, food, languages, fashion, etc. We have many people from different cultural backgrounds living here, such as the Native peoples – Aboriginals and Torres Strait Islanders, Europeans, Chinese, Indians, Africans, and many more different racial and ethnic groups. It is also the home of many different religions as discussed in the previous section.

For youth from migrant backgrounds, it is very easy to find migrant communities in your neighborhood. These could be helpful, as they could have people who are kind, and would help you settle down into daily life in the new country. It is common for these communities to have people who come from your own country of origin. Details of these gatherings can be found on the local council website or on community notice-boards. They offer great services at a cheap cost. The services include tutoring, counselling sessions, access to centers (libraries, community halls, youth centers, etc.), information about your suburb, etc.

The different multicultural groups in Australia have largely lived together in harmony compared with to migration and integration experiences of from other countries. However, there are still challenges with multiculturalism. Three of such situations are presented below – stereotyping, racism and discrimination. They are included in this book mainly for the reasons that our target audience (youth of migrant backgrounds) should be aware that they exist and should be proactive in seeking timely advice if they are faced with any issues.

Stereotyping: Many people in Australia generally view migrants as people who ran away from their homes to come here. A few people believe that migrants are people of good value if as they provide a service to the community. "Stereotyping" is when people form an instant opinion when they first see the person. This perception bias is generally untrue and can cause friction and turmoil. Due to stereotyping, people generally make fun and look down on migrant youth as those who can't cope with the academic standards and need to be put into intensive courses to master the basics. For example, if you are perceived as struggling with English language, you are expected to put some work into it via some kind of government-supported program. The expectation is that you will need it later on, and you could master it in one to two years, especially while you are still young.

This system may have worked for some people. But, *we all should not be put in one box*, i.e., "every migrant youth needs help with English Language." Hence on the street, at school and sometimes at home, you are approached with a mindset that you would require help with everyday communication. You may be currently experiencing this situation as a migrant youth (or later on), especially in an intimidating manner. Talk to your family, school teacher, counselor or chaplain, religious leader or a trusted adult if someone is making you uncomfortable. Don't keep it quiet! Don't keep it secret! Call it out!

Racism: Statistics show that many non-Anglo-Saxon people (such as Aboriginal people, Italians, Chinese, South Americans, Africans, Middle-easterners, etc.) have suffered racism. Racism can affect youth of migrant backgrounds, especially those going through high school, as the atmosphere in some schools may not be so pleasant. It is not uncommon for children to be mildly, or sometimes, even extremely racist. This situation could also well continue into working lives of youth of migrant backgrounds, with statistics showing that to get as many job interviews as an Anglo-Saxon applicant of the same qualifications and experience, Chinese people, for example, need to submit more applications. Such trends point to the fact that some forms of racism may still exist in Australia.

Youth of migrant backgrounds should stand up against racism in a non-aggressive and non-violent manner. We don't need to form youth gangs in order to address this issue. The wider community can (and should) also stand up against racism and increasingly support victims of racism.

It is also vital for victims to share how they feel about the situation, as this would be helpful in the healing process. They should not keep it in, but rather tell a trusted adult who can take proper action immediately.

Finally, the entire community and government at all levels should encourage and promote multicultural activities and targeted campaigns against racism.

Discrimination is the poor treatment of someone by virtue of their perceived class, wealth, social status, background, etc. This could happen in the workplace, at school, in public places or in restrooms. There are different types of discrimination, some of which are: racial discrimination, direct discrimination and indirect discrimination.

Racial discrimination is when someone treats you poorly depending on where you come from and the colour of your skin. This type of discrimination is most commonly found in high schools and at workplaces. For example, a waiter at a restaurant may decide to serve white Australian customers their meals first before attending to an African customer who has clearly been waiting longer. This would be an act of racial discrimination, as it would make the African customer feel unwelcome and underserved. The reverse could also happen i.e. given the African preferential treatment, maybe in an African nation.

Direct discrimination is when someone is treated less favorably because of their background or personal characteristics. As a youth, you may get some direct discrimination, but you won't experience it as much as racial discrimination and indirect discrimination.

Indirect discrimination is an unreasonable rule or policy that affects everyone but affects some more because of their personal traits and characteristics. This type of discrimination is most commonly found in workplaces, and occasionally in schools. This type of discrimination is the least noticeable type, and generally leaves the doer looking like they are not at fault. Although there are many laws about discrimination, it is not really considered a crime and victims as well as perpetrators generally keep quiet on the matter.

Some solutions for youth of migrant backgrounds against discrimination include – calling it out, standing up for yourself as far as possible, reaching out for support, especially by telling family members, teachers and/or other trusted persons. It is also important to take care of yourself and learn to cope and rise above such situations. The support networks mentioned above can provide help and guidance in all such circumstances and become places of comfort, safety and protection.

Unfortunately, some youth of migrant backgrounds are driven to explore options that are beyond the rule of law in order to protect themselves. Membership of gangs may present such opportunity. Indeed, the issue of youth gangs is worthy of mention because it has recently made news headlines in Australia (2016 – 2018) causing fear and intimidation in the wider community and of youth of migrant backgrounds themselves.

'Migrant Youth Gangs': A gang is generally an alliance of three or more people. Gangs are meant to be a group of people who share one thing in common, which could – the way they dress, the tattoos and piercings they have, the 'protection' they provide, etc. Gangs are now more prevalent than ever including those in schools. However, the term 'gang' is mainly used for a criminal organization involved in dubious activities. Gang members are often involved in illegal and criminal work that lands them in prison. This shows that joining a gang may not be very helpful in the long run, because you'll either get yourself in trouble or end up going to jail.

Gangs have been spreading around all over the society and most young people that join do so in order to have a sense of identity and belonging. They want to act 'cool' or to maybe try and fit in with the people around them. Joining a gang for the sake of fitting in or just trying to impress people could get you killed. If anything were to happen or a gun fight was to break out, as we have seen or heard over the news in a few cases, and you died were injured as a result, how do you think your family, your friends and everyone else connected to you would feel?

Some youth of migrant backgrounds may have joined gangs for protection. They may have thought that they could better protect themselves from issues such as stereotyping, racism and discrimination. They may have also been looking for validation. The conversations around migrant youth gangs in Australia have been very charged at times with fiery topics including the era of "middle-eastern gangs", "African gangs", etc.

More recently, we hear of "gangs of African descent" possibly after the fact that many of the youth involved were born here in Australia. This triggers some questions — "Why the need for stereotyping? And the emphasis on race and background like "African gang", "Middle-Eastern gang", "Lebanese gang", etc.? Why not just call them gangs?" Many a times, gangs and gang events are politicized and used as a bait and election-swerving tactic.

Is this the best way to approach the issue? Are these youth of migrant backgrounds not being further marginalized this way and possibly pushed

> *It is our responsibility as youth of migrant backgrounds to not get caught up with gangs because we can be manipulated for selfish reasons for fulfilling a political agenda, or for providing 'cheap' news to the media.*

further into the dark abyss? There must be better ways of stopping the unpleasant cycle, and of enhancing better integration.

However, it is primarily our responsibility as youth of migrant backgrounds to not get caught up with gangs because we can be manipulated for selfish reasons, for fulfilling a political agenda, or for providing 'cheap' news to the media. We need to know and appreciate the consequences of being involved. Many times, the risks are very high including exposure to illicit drugs, violence, crime and deaths, as well as separation from loved ones — families, friends and neighbours. Considering the fact that gangs are under police surveillance and watch 24/7, the youth joining one could get their names in the bad books and have their careers and future prospects ruined forever.

> *Please take further action/s if you think you need help with your mental health after reading this section or any other part of this book.*
>
> *In Australia, you can call Lifeline on 13 11 14 or Beyond Blue on 1300 224 636 where mental illness or related concerns may be involved and deserves emergency action. Do not hesitate to call 000 for emergency police and/or ambulance, if necessary.*
>
> *Readers in other countries should call equivalent emergency contacts in their countries, as applicable.*

Australia has opened its doors and embraced people of all races, languages and cultures. The country's multiculturalism has been widely acclaimed as one of the best globally. Yes, there are challenges, but we believe the opportunities for youth of migrant backgrounds significantly outweigh these challenges.

2.4 Opportunities for Youth in Australia

There are so many opportunities available in Australia for young people including those of migrant backgrounds. They include: high-quality education, better standard of living, social and welfare support, youth employment opportunities, extra-curricular opportunities, community support groups and the freedom to be the best you can be.

There is no single scale that sufficiently measures the "standard of living"; however, a summary view can be obtained by considering a range of indicators. The term could mean different things to different people. You could consider it to mean "average salary" of persons in the employment sector, in an economic sense or "quality of life" that people generally enjoy, in a broader socio-economic sense.

A research study conducted by the United Nations (UN) in December 2015, reports that Australia is ranked as the second-best country in the world (only behind Norway) for its quality of life on three factors: economy, education and life expectancy (The Sydney Morning Herald, 18 Dec 2015 retrieved from https://www.smh.com.au/business/the-economy/australia-ranks-secondbest-in-the-world-for-quality-of-life-un-study-says-20151218-glqi0l.html 1 June 2019). The research also states that Australians can expect to live on average to about eighty-two and a half years of age, have thirteen years of schooling on an average and enjoy a gross annual income of $58,618 per person.

Social and welfare support for young people and their families is another incredible opportunity available in Australia. The quality of the outdoor environment (lakes, beaches, gardens, reserves, trails, etc.), limited criminal activity and high regard for public safety, access to world class healthcare systems and networks, and availability of essential social services — are very good relative to other countries in the world.

> *The opportunities for young people in Australia are numerous and diverse, established to this shining standard over the years as the country developed.*

Other social and welfare services offered in Australia that are of benefit to youth (directly or indirectly) include counseling and advocacy services, and family assistance benefits "Part A & B" — which is a form of government aid to assist families with children between the ages of birth to 15 years. These payments are administered by Centrelink, which is a part of the Department of Home Affairs, and are tested against incomes of families to ensure that the support reaches those who need it the most. Youth allowances are provided to young people of 16 – 24 years of age to provide ongoing support for studying, apprenticeship, employment search and even for those who cannot work for any reason or those who are unable to hold employment.

The opportunities for young people in Australia are numerous and diverse, established to this shining standard over the years as the country developed. Some of these will be detailed in the coming sections of this handbook, which include high-quality education and career pathways, advancement in technology, as well as fast and reliable internet connectivity and related social media and gaming.

The benefits, tchallenges and lessons associated with these opportunities will also be highlighted especially from the viewpoints, experiences and observations of LiME youth. Hopefully, this will provide some useful insights, wisdom and challenges to the readers of this book (especially new and emerging youth of migrant backgrounds, like us) while also providing adequate triggers for relevant actions to build great futures for young people.

Reflection 2.0:

- How do you see your place in this Country? How do you intend to take advantage of the opportunities of being in the country – for yourself, your family and your community? How will you contribute to the growth of the country as well?

  _____
  _____
  _____

- How much do you know about the history and indigenous people of this country? Why do you think it is important to know, respect and learn from this history?

  _____
  _____
  _____

- What does multiculturalism mean to you (before and after reading this chapter)? How do you feel as a resident and person of migrant background? Do you feel valued? Do you feel you belong? Going forward, what will be your attitude towards stereotyping, racism, discrimination, and youth gangs? How will you be an influence of positive changes, where necessary?

  _____
  _____
  _____

3.0 Education Pathways

Keyshiaa Menezes

Education is the cornerstone of the Australian society. It is a well-established and time-honoured institution that brings pride to everyone involved – students, their families, educators, the government and the community at large. Australia's integrated education system is supported by the Australian Qualifications Framework (AQF), a national policy for regulated qualifications across schools, vocational, educational, and training centres (VET) and centres for higher education.

Education is very important in Australia. It is compulsory for every child in Australia to be in school for the period beginning of from the year in which the child turns five years and six months of age, and until the end of the year in which he or she turns 17 years and six months or 18 years of age (www.education.wa.edu.au).

LiMErs in Education Mode

There are an assortment of schools and places of formal education in Australia of every type. A 2016 research report by The Australian Trade and Investment Commission (www.austrade.gov.au) indicates that there are over 6,600 public schools, over 1700 catholic schools, over 1,000 independent schools and over 460 schools for special needs in the country. The split between primary, secondary and combined schools are 6,200+, 1400+ and 1300+ respectively. The same report states that there as 43 universities with estimated 1 million students and 5000+ Registered Training Organisation (RTOs) with about 4.5 million students.

Check out the Australian Government Department of Education website (www.education.gov.au) and those of the various states (e.g. www.education.wa.edu.au for WA) for more details on various aspects of education in Australia including the different curriculums and standards.

3.1 Levels of Education in Australia

This section highlights the various levels of education in Australia, the associated conditions of learning and the expected outcomes involved. Again, details can be obtained from the relevant Department of Education websites presented in the previous section.

Kindergarten, Primary and Secondary School Education

Kindergarten to Year 10 education is compulsory in Australia. Thereafter, each student must make a choice between ATAR or General Pathway as well as selecting associated subjects if the student chooses to continue to Year 11 and/or 12. *ATAR stands for Australian Tertiary Admission Rank -*

the scoring system used for university admission in Australia. Queensland uses the OP (Overall Position) system. General Pathway, on the other hand, is the equivalent of the Vocational Education & Training (VET) pathway that leads to admission into Technical and Further Education (TAFE).

The Western Australian Certificate of Education (WACE) is awarded to senior secondary school students who satisfy its requirements. It is a senior secondary certificate recognised nationally as per AQF requirements for this level of education. Generally, students are expected to successfully complete two years of senior secondary study to achieve the WACE. Refer to the WA Department of Education website (www.education.wa.edu.au) and its equivalents in other states for details about the requirements for the awarding of the senior secondary certificate and other aspects of education at K-12 levels.

VET / TAFE Education

TAFE is an alternative to university which provides training in job-related and technical skills and falls under the tertiary education and training segment. It covers a large number of careers and industries, such as construction, apprenticeships for trades, office work, retail, nursing, hospitality, technology etc. Qualifications awarded after completing the education at this level, as per AQF requirements, include Certificates I, II, III and IV, as well as Diplomas and Advanced Diplomas.

Refer to AQF website (https://www.aqf.edu.au/aqf-levels) for the knowledge and skills associated with the various qualifications and applications of these knowledge and skills in the workplace.

University Education

University is a tertiary education which on completion will earn students the qualifications including: Bachelor's Degree, Bachelor (Honours), Graduate Certificate, Graduate Diploma, Master's and Doctoral Degrees. Some common courses of study in Australian universities are in the areas of science, management, commerce, humanities, engineering, architecture, law and health sciences. Students sometimes choose to enroll in a double or combined Bachelor's Degree program which leads to the awarding of two Bachelor's Degrees. This is most common in the fields of arts, commerce, law and science (www.studyinaustralia.gov.au).

3.2 Some Important Aspects of K-12 Education in Western Australia

This next section provides highlights of some specific aspects of K-12 levels of education including the topics of catchment areas, NAPLAN, Specialist programs, GATE and Homeschooling.

Catchment Areas

In Australia, when you go to a public school, it must be in your catchment area or "Local Neighbourhood Zone". This is not the case with private schools, where you have the freedom to choose which one to go to.

However, entry and stay in most private schools will depend on meeting the school's requirements over and above those specified by the Department of Education. These could include payment of fees, adherence to the school's rules and values (like faith-based schools), etc. Thus, most families would choose schools for their children based on affordability, nearness to home and/or work, preferences for faith-based education, record of academic performance, school's specialised programs such as sports teams, school's reputation etc.

NAPLAN

'NAPLAN' stands for National Assessment Program — Literacy and Numeracy. It is an annual national assessment taken by all students in the years 3, 5, 7 and 9. All students in these year levels are expected to participate in this test which assesses students' reading, writing, language (spelling, grammar and punctuation) and numeracy skills. It is administered by the Australian Curriculum, Assessment and Reporting Authority (ACARA). The overall purpose of NAPLAN is to provide a snapshot of a student's current reading, writing, language and numeracy aptitude.

OLNA (https://www.education.wa.edu.au/olna)

OLNA is an online literacy and numeracy assessment. It is an assessment that students need to pass to successfully meet the required standard in for Literacy and Numeracy. Students who have not achieved Band 8 in the year 9 component of NAPLAN are required to take the OLNA. The

Education Pathways

assessment requires students to demonstrate skills that are regarded as essential to meet the demands of daily life. The assessment occurs each year in March and September for young people in of years 10, 11 and 12. Once the participants have passed the minimum standard, they are no longer required to sit take the assessment again. There are six opportunities to pass this assessment. Check the Department of Education website (www.education.wa.edu.au) for more details as required.

Specialised Programs

Some schools run specialised programs including those in the areas of sports, arts and applied sciences. These approved specialised programs give students real-world skills and a head start in at achieving their career goals. Many of them are linked to sporting and industry bodies as well as training organisations, with the aim of giving opportunities to participating students to gain industry-recognised qualifications. Graduates of such programs have gone on to become professional athletes, cinematographers, fashion designers, marine biologists, sports coaches, etc.

GATE

'GATE' stands for Gifted and Talented Secondary Selective Entry Program. It is offered at 20 select public schools in WA including a fully selective academic school (Perth Modern School), an arts school, a regional school, and an online program for country students. Screening and selection is administered via a competitive Academic Selective Entrance Test (ASET) which has 4 parts – (1) reading comprehension, (2) communicating ideas in writing, (3) quantitative reasoning and (4) Abstract reasoning. The applications for the test usually open in October, and close the following year in February. Students whose applications are accepted are notified and they take the test in March. Notifications of the outcomes of the test are sent out in May, successful candidates are interviewed subsequently and offers are made by June in view of commencement of the GATE program the following year.

> Education can provide anyone with a useful platform to develop self and find employment. Everyone deserves a good education. This has been my experience and that of my peers.

Homeschooling

Homeschooling refers to the education of children at home by their parents. Also referred to as home education, this type of education has become an increasingly attractive option for many families in Australia. Under the nation's School Education Act 1999, parent/s that wish to be fully responsible for delivering their children's education program can register with the applicable Department of Education as home educators. This means the parents are in charge of educating their children during their compulsory education period. They will be responsible for completing their wards' registrations into the programs, planning these programs, obtaining all required materials, and delivering and monitoring the programs to the specified standards. Homeschooling parents will also be required to demonstrate their children's progress on an ongoing basis.

Education can provide anyone with a useful platform to develop self and find employment. Everyone deserves good education. This has been my experience and that of my peers.

Reflection 3.0:

- Why do you think education is so important, to the extent that it is compulsory for every child to go to school in some Countries (including Australia)? Think about it and write down a few points to capture your thoughts.

  _____
  _____
  _____

- Where do you want to be many years from now in terms of career, family, influence, and recreation? Do you know the educational pathway that will lead you there? Do you readily seek for help and guidance with regards to this situation (from school, family, community leaders)?

  _____
  _____
  _____

- Do you know that in a Country like Australia (and many others as well), it is never too late to get back on the pathway to your success? Do you know that there are also built-in flexibilities to provide options along the way? Write down some thoughts on where you are right now. Write down action steps you will undertake to ensure success including where and how you will seek for help, where applicable.

  _____
  _____
  _____

4.0 Youth & Technology

Ify Okiwelu and Joshuaa Menezes

Technology is the 'science of craft', from the Greek word 'τέχνη', 'techne', which means 'art, skill, cunning of hand'; and '-λογία', '-logia'. It which is the collection of techniques, skills, methods and processes used in the production of goods or services, or in the accomplishment of objectives (Wikipedia.org). This means that such technology has been put through tests to see if it suits peoples' needs and that it is safe and robust to survive daily use.

It also means that it has been designed to help simplify tasks that humans do. For example, a spoon was designed to use to pick up food and insert it into our mouths without making a mess. A mobile phone was invented to help humans to communicate through a world of digital connections. Technology in Australia has largely influenced youth and young adults, and the reverse is true as well: Youth have influenced the types and level of use of technology and how it impacts our lives.

LiMErs in AI & Robotics Session

4.1 Technology for Schools and Learning

Schools and education centres use technology to guide people and help them understand the various different learning pathways available to them. Here, technology is used to attend to the needs of the students and learners as well as the educators and staff.

In universities and learning places, they have courses that you can study, such as computers and graphic design, video games and game design, artificial intelligence, robotics, intelligent construction, etc. Jobs and careers are also on the increase in these areas of technology and its applications.

4.2 Technology for Play, Entertainment and Everyday Living

Access to technology is also on the rise. There are lots of video games on various platforms – phones, tablets, TVs, etc. Read more about the internet, social media and gaming in the next chapter.

Did you know that you can go to a local library and get a membership card to access computers? While there, you could also borrow gaming devices for entertainment, if they have that facility available.

Digital technology comes in many forms such as, computers, phones, gaming consoles and smart devices. These things assist us in many ways, like the computer that I we used to type down and document this important and very informative book.

Also, there are gaming consoles with games especially designed for youth, which are targeted at multiplayer audiences. Although these are great, sometimes, it they can also get out of hand.

Virtual assistants are tremendously useful, like Cortana, Siri, Alexa and Google. You can ask them questions and they can answer back with relevant information. The accuracy of voice recognition is improving considerably as well.

4.3 Technology for Work and Business

Technology has revolutionised the way we look at the world and how we perform our jobs and tasks. There are big- and established companies like IBM, Apple, Microsoft, etc. and, now, new and emerging companies like Tesla and Oppo.

Technology also drives innovation with it. Examples of this can be seen in Surface Pros and convertible laptops that allow for creativity. Artificial Intelligence (AI) and machine learning are technologies that are changing the world around us at breakneck pace. Not only do they make our tasks easier they also add a lot of creative value. And let's face it, they make our work a lot faster and a lot more efficient. Before 1972, people used handwritten letters to interact with each other, but when email was invented, it became a quick and efficient way to send messages across.

Over time, technological companies have evolved and adapted to the changing demands of the modern age by being innovative and inventive. Some companies, like Nokia and Motorola, have fallen back and are obsolete now. Back in the day, Nokia and Motorola were the Apple and Samsung of today. Suddenly, both companies have been forced to either quickly adapt or fall out of the phone industry all together.

4.4 Technology for the Future

Technology is influencing the way we prepare for our future as individuals and community of people. One of the most discussed things in today's society is the increasing awareness and reality of electric cars. It is an advancement in technology and it is also quite an exceptional one since it is "green technology" that doesn't give out any emissions that contribute to the greenhouse effect.

Compared to an internal combustion engine (I.C.E), these cars have a big battery that drives the DC motors and powers the car. They are faster, more efficient and cheaper to run compared to a petrol / diesel vehicle. As an added bonus, you can plug the car in to at home and power it. Charging is can also be free if you have solar panels installed. Imagine not having to pay massive repair and fuel costs with an electric car that only has one (1) moving part compared to the I.C.E.'s minimum of three hundred (300) moving parts.

Then imagine the ultimate technological reality of a completely "driverless" electric car that too will be available to us in the near future!

4.5 Youth and Technology: The Balance

There are numerous advantages of technology. It enhances education and learning; it provides multiple options for play, social interactions, work and everyday living; as well as preparing us for an exciting future. But there are also challenges and pitfalls with technology. For example, the internet and social media have been known for having many bad influences, like creating false notions, promoting negativity, body harming self-image, spreading pornography, encouraging unhealthy sleep patterns, creating avenues for cyberbullying, etc.

> *Let technology support your life; but don't allow it to take over.*

A recent statistic from the Children's eSafety Commission shows that 19% of young people aged between 14-17 years have either been harassed or bullied online and 17% of them have been exposed to inappropriate content in one single calendar month alone.

An AUKOS study in 2011 showed that 13% of children in Australia had been cyber-bullied. What is more shocking is that this figure is more than double of the average of 25 European countries combined at 6%. Parents must get actively involved in increasing the cyber safety and security for their children. Youth themselves can (and should) also take responsibility for their own safety. Visit the eSafety Government page for more information. These sites offer information and resources about cyber safety, how to manage cyber issues as well as educational materials for pre-teens and young teens on how to manage cyber issues if any arise.

Youth & Technology

Technology can be good and bad. It has its challenges, just like many good things in life. The key is awareness of the technologies you're interacting with including understanding why you are using them and how to use them. It is important to ensure moderation in use. Let technology support your life; but don't allow it to take over.

Do you know that in a Country like Australia (and many others as well), it is never too late to get back on the pathway to your success? Do you know that there are also built-in flexibilities to provide options along the way? Write down some thoughts on where you are right now. Write down action steps you will undertake to ensure success including where and how you will seek for help, where applicable.

Reflection 4.0:

- How can we use technology to learn better?

  _____
  _____
  _____
  _____
  _____

- "Let technology support your life; but don't allow it to take over." How do you intend to strike the right balance for you?

  _____
  _____
  _____
  _____
  _____

- Where do you see the next big technological advancement? How do you position yourself to be part of the discovery? Think about it and write down some few thoughts.

  _____
  _____
  _____
  _____
  _____

5.0 Internet, Social Media and Gaming

Efe Osaghae, Odaro Osaghae and Victor Komaiya

Internet, social media and gaming have become a part of the daily lives of young people across the globe including Australian youth. Before getting into the discussion on why, it is important to first provide a little understanding of what they are.

Internet is a system of interconnected networks where pieces of technology can communicate with any other technology that is connected to it. Video games, are games played online that come in the form of console games, computer games and also phone apps. And, social media are virtual networks that allow their users to create and share their own content and communicate with each other.

LiME in Session

5.1 Why Internet, Social Media and Gaming?

The usage of social media, gaming and the internet is commonplace in Australia. Many things are influenced by social media, gaming and the internet. Jobs such as software developers and programmers use gaming in their work. Marketing managers, business owners and even people who work in public relationship jobs need social media to operate. That's why social media and gaming are so important.

The internet is the most important of the three. Without the internet, you won't have access to social media or video games anyway. The internet first started after the development and production of electronic computers around the 1950's. At first, its purpose was to have a defense network that would work during the nuclear war. Now, it has evolved into our most relied-upon resource.

There are so many reasons you cannot live without the internet, for example, jobs. You don't have to be tech savvy to rely upon the internet for your work. Office workers must use the internet and even job seekers use it to find jobs. Corporates use the internet to pitch advertisements and introduce new products, product features and services. Nearly all schools have switched to internet-relying devices such as Chromebooks, laptops and MacBooks. By using these, they reduce the usage of paper-based notebooks and textbooks. These devices also make every day work and tasks easier for both the teachers and students.

Internet, Social Media and Gaming

Shopping is also a big thing on the internet. Most people rely on online shopping for most of their needs — gifts, groceries, jewellery, electronics and clothes.

Lastly, the internet powers video games and social media. While some video games are console-based and don't necessarily need the internet, now there are online game stores even for consoles, which must be connected to the internet to work. Social media also needs the internet browsing. This is why the internet is so vital.

Social media is also a topic that could draw the attention of just about anyone. A network that has revolutionised the way we connect and communicate will, of course, draw the attention of many. Everyone wants to have their say and have their views acknowledged. But regardless of your stance on the matter, most opinions - whether extreme or neutral - have some pros and cons (as you will read in a later section below).

Social media 'users' is a term used in reference to people who own an account and use social media. They can register on a number of platforms (see next section for the different social media networks and platforms). Users must often be over 13 years of age, mainly for legal reasons and for reasons of security and protection. However, many parents view social media as a bad influence and may choose to prohibit their ward's use. Some parents don't see a need for social media, and may limit its use for entertainment purposes only. They believe this will keep their child away from potentially harmful content. However, others may be more embracing of social media and allow their children unrestricted.

Most times, it is challenging for parents, teachers and other caregivers to draw the line. One thing is useful though: seeking a reasonable understanding of the various types of social media platforms and delving into their pros and cons. This is the focus of the next two sections.

5.2 Different Types of Social Media and Gaming

There are so many types of social media and gaming platforms these days. Some have come and faded away so quickly, while others are being used over a long period of time and are still on in demand. The points presented below are mainly based on the more popular types.

Social Media

Facebook/Instagram:

Who doesn't have a Facebook account these days? Even if they don't use their account actively, they definitely have one and it's hard to find anyone who has a smartphone and no Facebook application installed on it. It is really is used worldwide and is often a tool to connect us with family and friends and keep connections alive.

Instagram, a very similar app, is often the platform of choice for many teens and young adults. Both these businesses — Facebook and Instagram — are operated by Mark Zuckerberg who founded Facebook. Both Instagram and Facebook, allow users to 'post' and interact with content — text, pictures and videos. Followers of an account can tap the 'like' button to let the account owner know they enjoyed the post or leave a comment that the user can see and respond to. People can stay in the loop with what their friends and family are doing (or more accurately, what they choose to post), which is a great segue into my next point.

Followers of an account can only see what that user chooses to post, meaning users are in control of how others perceive them - which is both good and bad. For example, say a particular user is going through a tough time; suppose they are battling depression. But if the user constantly makes posts of him/her looking happy and content, it gives out a false impression that life is 'peachy'. If you aren't a close friend and only follow the account, it's likely you wouldn't have a clue about the realities the user is actually struggling with. But say this user has a large social media presence, meaning that he/she has more followers than an average user. Now another problem arises - the many followers of only see the 'perfect moments' of the user's life and piece together a thoroughly misconstrued image of perfection. They wish their life could also be as 'perfect'. But they remain unaware that the user with over 10k-followers and 3,000 likes on each of his/her posts is going through as many problems as the person with 100 followers getting only about 20 likes.

Now 'likes' - what's so good about them? Why are they such a big deal? Let me tell you a secret: unless you're using social media for business (which we'll go into later), 'likes' mean nothing. Likes (depicted by a

> Likes on social media ... what do they mean? Sign of appreciation? What do you do with the likes? Can they be cashed in? Do they make you a better human being?

thumbs up icon on Facebook) are a way to of showing appreciation, support or enjoyment of a post.

"But I thought likes meant nothing?" - Well yes, they are a sign of appreciation and such; they have meaning, but they don't equate to anything. A friend may like your post because they thought it was a nice picture, but then what do you do with that like? It's not currency, it can't be cashed in; it doesn't make you a better human being; you don't gain any new knowledge; and in most cases, it doesn't make you any more applicable for a job. Still, though, the question remains: why are likes a big deal?

Well, for many people - myself included - seeing people liking our posts makes us feel good. It's almost as if every time one of your followers likes or loves your post, they're telling you, "Good job. This is cool." - when, in fact, some people scroll their feed so fast, they're liking whatever's on their screen without actually getting into the details of what they just liked.

Often, we get so caught up in the number of likes we're getting, it becomes a quotient of our self-esteem or self-worth. If for whatever reason we don't get as many likes as we think we deserve, it quickly becomes an issue. If people you consider friends don't like your posts, they become your enemy enemies for the day. It seems easy to say, "Yeah, I won't let the number of likes I get affect me", but it truly is harder easier said than done.

Suppose a user posts a picture of themselves in a meadow, where their face isn't visible - say this post gets 200 likes. Now, the same user posts a selfie, in which their face is fully visible - it gets 150 likes. Now the user is left to wonder about the discrepancy in the number of likes. The user may think that their followers didn't enjoy the picture of their face as much and "maybe people think I'm ugly" becomes the theme. This kind of thinking that is so common in the social media space is, of course, detrimental to the user's self-image.

In terms of privacy, Instagram seems safer as it's seen to be more child-friendly. Facebook requires users to be over 18 years of age, so and Instagram is more or less the same thing. Both have customisable privacy settings; however, many consider Instagram to be more intuitive - the app is even preset for privacy. Upon creating an account, all of the user's content is visible only to those who follow their account; the user receives requests from other accounts but can choose to accept or decline any request, keeping relative control of who sees their posts. Privacy settings can be personalised even further to include posts and stories (a kind of 24-hour expiring post) that can only be viewed by 'close friends' - a customisable list of friends (from your followers) you deem closer than your wider range of followers. But And in the same manner, Instagram and Facebook accounts can be made completely public.

The content of public Instagram (IG) and Facebook (FB) accounts can be seen by anyone with internet access - you don't need to have a social media account of any kind to view public IG or FB pages. This feature, easily enabled by the tap of 2 or 3 buttons, compromises safety in a few ways. The most obvious is the account visibility by literally anyone - friends, family and felons alike. Public accounts also have no way of accessing their followers. The public account may amass a greater number of followers than a private account, but it becomes very difficult to keep track of who exactly is following you.

In the world we live in, any job can earn you a living if you know how to market your goods or services properly. Social media influencers are paid to promote products, services or other content (workouts, diet plans, etc.), and such. In this scenario, the more the followers an account has, the greater the number of people the promotional post will reach. Put simply, social media influencers amass as many followers as they can through both genuine and not-so-genuine means.

That said, let this not discourage you — I am we are only advising caution. As I we mentioned earlier, Facebook and Instagram definitely have their positives. Sharing funny posts with friends can often end up becoming the highlight of our day. The simplicity of the 'Direct Messaging' (DM) system makes finding and texting friends easy. Yes, it is not the same thing as meeting in person, but texting serves a different purpose - it is not supposed to be a substitute for face-to-face interaction. It often sustains the connection between friends, allowing them to keep in touch.

Twitter:

Twitter allows you to send post a short text message which is called a tweet. It is like sending a message to the world.

Snapchat:

Snapchat is an app that allows you to chat with your friends through pictures. It can also allow you to check what's making news, what's trending and what's happening around the world. Like Instagram, Snapshat is very popular with teenagers and young adults.

WhatsApp:

WhatsApp is a communication app that allows people from around the world to communicate via messaging and VOIP calls. Just like the Facebook Messenger, it is a cheap option of verbal communication across the globe, in that two or more people on either side of the call only need an internet connection to connect via WhatsApp.

Skype:

Skype is owned by Microsoft and is one of the more popular video networking platforms where you can even have group calls with a number of people located anywhere in the world at the same time.

Gaming

Statistics show that 95% of Australian homes have at least one device dedicated to playing video games. Some of the most popular video games that are played in Australia are:

- Grand Theft Auto 5 • Fortnite • Destiny 2 • Apex Legends • Minecraft
- Mortal Kombat 11 • Fifa 19 • Far Cry 5 • NBA 2K 19 • Resident Evil 2
- PUB G • Leagues of Legends • Overwatch.

Some popular video game publishers are: • Sony Interactive Entertainment • Microsoft • Ubisoft • Activision • Rockstar Games • Electronic Arts (EA) • Nintendo

5.3 Advantages and Disadvantages of Internet, Social Media and Gaming

Internet, social media and gaming have their advantages and disadvantages, like other things of in life. Some of them will be presented in this section. The points presented here are mainly related to social media and videogaming since these two are the most prominent subjects in the context of this book.

Social Media

Social media is the most debated topic, and there are many pros and cons to consider.

The first and foremost advantage of social media is **connectivity**. People from anywhere can connect with anyone, regardless of their location, age or background. The beauty of social media is that you can connect with anyone to learn and share your thoughts.

Social media has a lot of **educational** benefits for students and teachers. It is very easy to learn from others who are knowledgeable, experts or professionals in an area of interest. You can follow anyone to learn from them and enhance your knowledge about the subject area. Regardless of your location and background, you can educate yourself, without having to pay for it.

You can share your issues with the wider community to and get **help**. Whether it is receiving help in terms of money or advice, you can get it all from the network you are connected with.

The main advantage of social media is that you can get instant **updates** about the latest happenings around in the world. Most of the time, television and print media, are delayed in conveying the news.

Whether you have a brick and mortar store or an online business, you can **promote** your business to a large audience on social media. And, you can use social media to refine your reach and connect with the right audience.

Social media can also be used for promoting **noble causes**. For example, to promote an NGO, social welfare activities and donations for people or causes. People use social media to make donations and it can be a quick way to of sending help in such situations.

> *The internet, social media and gaming have many pros and cons. How do you take advantage of the pros and minimize the cons?*

Social media also creates **awareness** and encourages **innovation**. From farmers to teachers, students to lawyers every individual can benefit from social media.

Social media also can help governments and security agencies in catching criminals and for **fighting crime.**

There are also disadvantages associated with social media. Many children and teenagers have become victims of **cyberbullying** over social media channels. Since anyone can create a fake account and do anything without being traced, it has become quite easy for people to bully others. There have been cases where such crimes have driven the victims to attempt suicide.

Threats via social media are also prevalent. Intimidating messages and rumours can hurt your reputation and compromise you.

Personal data and privacy can easily be **hacked** and shared on the internet, which can result in financial losses and loss of self-esteem and confidence.

Similarly, **identity theft** is another big issue that can result in great losses. Perpetuators hack into their victim's personal accounts, assume their identity and transact in their name, compromising their personal credentials and data.

The **addictive** part of social media is very bad and can disturb personal lives as well. Teenagers are the most affected by addiction to social media. They can get heavily involved and eventually cut off from society. In many cases, addiction can result in experiencing issues such as depression and anxiety.

There are also cases where individuals **scam** others and commit **fraud** through social media.

Video Games

One advantage of video games is **education**, as studies show that many games provide learning opportunities to their players. The players can then apply what they have learnt in from the video game to their everyday life. Building games are examples of this; building games such as Minecraft are commonly used in primary schools.

Various action games are used for **military training** and capacity building for skills such as shooting, defense, survival, etc. Video games, in this context, provide less expensive opportunity and near-real experience for virtual training ahead of the real battle situation.

Another advantage of video games is **teamwork**; many online video games require users to work together with their friends and sometimes even complete strangers. This collaboration builds many life-skills in the players.

Yet, another advantage of video games is **improved brain function and coordination skills** which improve and while managing the different buttons and controls on the remote. They also improve our decision-making skills.

Video games can be physically engaging and help you **exercise** your body. The former classic Nintendo Wii included physical activity in the game that encouraged kids to play the sport from their living room. Even the former trend of Pokémon Go required users to go out and walk around to chase their Pokémon. Geocaching is also similar to Pokémon Go being a real-life treasure hunt game.

On the flip side of the coin, video games can sometimes encourage **violence**. The most popular video games involve fighting, shooting and hunting. These games can lead to situations where the brain accepts and adapts to the constant violence that can trigger players to carry out acts of violence in real life.

One of the biggest disadvantages of video games is the risk of **addiction**. According to Game Quitter (https://gamequitters.com/), 3-4% of the gamers are addicted to the games they play. People who have poor impulse control or those who struggle to fit in with their peers are more likely to become addicted.

> *Internet, social media and gaming: it's about striking the right balance*

Addiction can also lead to another situation called **social replacement**. Many gamers end up replacing their social time with game time or online communication time. This can reduce their social skills and can even make them **susceptible to cyberbullying** through online game sites.

5.4 Striking the Right Balance

There are many good aspects of internet, social media and gaming as shown in this chapter. However, it is also very challenging to be confronted with the associated risks and the fact that there have been deaths where the root causes were traced to involvement in internet-driven social media and gaming. They can indeed influence your social life, work and daily lifestyle as a young migrant. If social media and gaming are used rightly, they can improve how you go about in our everyday life.

Internet, Social Media and Gaming

Contributing to this chapter has made us reflect once again, the good, the challenges and the lessons in the use of internet, social media and gaming. The situation calls for striking the right balance as youth and especially as migrant youth. We have some much to contribute to life and meaningfulness of future generations that we cannot afford to have our involvements in these platforms take so much out of us, that they should.

Remarkably, our parents, teachers and other care-givers can hardly monitor and track us effectively these days. Really, our generation outsmarts theirs when it comes to things like these. Nevertheless, the negative impacts of overindulgence in internet, social media and gaming affect us directly, and much more than them. Let us own the responsibility of striking and maintaining the right balance.

> *Please take further action/s if you think you need help with your mental health after reading this Chapter or any other part of this book. In Australia, you can call Lifeline on 13 11 14 or Beyond Blue on 1300 224 636 where mental illness or related concerns may be involved and deserves emergency action. Do not hesitate to call 000 for emergency police and/orambulance, if necessary. Readers in other counties should call equivalent emergency contacts in their countries, as applicable.*

Reflection 5.0:

- How much time do you spend on social media and/or gaming? Do you consider this healthy for you? Are you doing it safely (for you and others)? Take some time to write down a few thoughts

    _____

    _____

    _____

- Have you thought about the advantages and disadvantages of internet, social media and gaming as presented in this book? What steps would you undertake to maximise the advantages and minimise the disadvantages for you?

    _____

    _____

    _____

- What is the right balance for you? How do you intend to strike this balance on a practical level?

    _____

    _____

    _____

6.0 Youth & Finances

Marcus Wilson, Osamu Ekhator and Saskia Wilson

6.1 Introduction to Financial Education

Money is a difficult topic, especially for youth. At this age, we have a want to be independent, but also a want for more toys, more gadgets, more movies, more things. The big questions are: How can you tie independence and all these *wants* together? How do you learn about money? What is the best way to acquire it? And when you do how do you keep it?

> *If you learn how to save money whilst you're young it will be easier as you get older*

Finance is a big part of our lives and learning how to make and manage is essential, especially in today's world of instant gratification. Without money, you can't buy things you want or need.

Starting early is one of the best things that you can do for yourself. If you can learn how to save money whilst you're young, it will be easier as you get older.

LiMErs in Financial Education Session

6.2 Saving Money

Now, you have a basic understanding of what money is. How can it be used and what can you do with it? You are going to need a place to store it. A place that is safe and secured. A place that is worth storing such a valuable resource.

Piggy Banks Vs. Savings Accounts: There are many ways to store your money: in a money box, in a piggy bank or even under the mattress. But there is a much better way to store your money; in a place where it will be safe. That place is called a savings account in the bank or some kind of financial institution that have the resources to secure your money for you, pay you back an interest while they have your money and they are being regulated by government. This method is used by almost everyone, and for a good reason.

6.3 Starting a Money-Saving Habit

Now that you have a place to store your money, you will need to routinely add to it. Whilst this may sound simple, there are many things in the world that you might want to have, and these things will cost money.

With all of these distractions, it can be quite difficult to set aside some money to save. But it's essential to begin now, because when you are older and you have your own house, car and family, the expenses start to pile up. You will need to pay for petrol, water, electricity, gas bills, the list goes on. If you begin now, you will create a habit that will stick with you for the rest of your life. This means that if you teach yourself a money-saving habit now, when you are older you will be used to saving.

6.4 The Fear of Missing Out

Whilst you are saving money, and striving not to waste your time or your resources, there are many things that may distract you, and one of those things is the fear of missing out.

Your friends may have invited you to a movie that you don't really want to see, or requested that you come along to a restaurant that you do not care for. It's important that you never waste your time doing something you don't want to. If you don't like the food at the restaurant, don't go. If you don't want to watch that movie, don't go. Otherwise, if you do not enjoy yourself, it will be a waste of two of your most precious resources: money and time.

> *Don't allow FOMO to cause you to truly miss out.*

It is also important that you try to minimise your insecurities. You shouldn't worry whether your peers think that you are fun or not. It should not matter what other people think of you.

6.5 Become Independent and Entrepreneurial

Many children, these days, especially in developed countries such as Australia, get everything from their parents; their toys, their gadgets, their computers, their mobile phones, an allowance, etc. All of this is well and all, but if you do not learn to develop with the resources that your parents give you, their time and their money, you will not grow.

Learn to save the money that your parents give you. Learn to make more money with the resources that they make open to you. It is important that you learn to become independent at an early age; that you learn to do things for yourself. Those children who just take their parents' resources and spend it on things that will instantly gratify, will not be successful in the long run, while those who choose to invest and save their parents resources will. This is a key principle of entrepreneurship. This involves being innovative in ways of creating opportunities for ourselves. For example, we have embraced the school-based banking knowing that every dollar we are saving now has the potential to become big investments for us later on in our futures. We also take initiative of 'working' for our mums and dads including doing extra house chores for extra allowances (and we save some of these as well) thereby developing a culture of hard work.

Finally, financial education is a big part of our ongoing development. Thankfully, LiME has provided us with fun-driven ways of learning financial principles.

> *Get educated! Financial education pays.*

6.6 Get Educated!

Financial education helps us in our daily lives. With the right help and mentors, like we have at LiME, it will be easier to learn about it and use it every day.

Even as a child, there are many things that you can do to prepare yourself for the future, such as starting a money-saving habit and setting up a savings account. There are many ways to achieve your goals, and it just becomes easier with money. As stated before, money can do many things: it can bring people out of poverty, it can fix climate change and global warming, and it can change the world.

Reflection 6.0:

- What is your attitude towards finance? Why is financial education important for you? How wealthy do you want to be? Take some time to write down a few thoughts.

  _____
  _____
  _____

- What are your financial goals? When should one start saving some money? 3 years, 13 years, 18 years? 25 years? 50 years? 75 years? . . . For a young person: do you think everything depends on your parents (and you don't need to bother)?

  _____
  _____
  _____

- How do you ensure that FOMO does not make you really miss out? Think about it and write down a few points.

  _____
  _____
  _____

7.0 Youth and mental Health

King-David Oyewopo

The topic of mental health is a difficult one to discuss even one-to-one, so it becomes more challenging to air a view in a book — by a youth. However, the issues associated with mental health and illness deserve all necessary attention including conversations within youth groups. After all, the stigma and secrecy associated with this topic have done more harm than good (if any good at all).

The texts in this chapter are completely my views — some original, and others, based on research and observations over my last 16 years of living in this world. I am not a specialist, nor do I claim to know so much of this subject. The aim of expressing my views here is to lend a voice as well as provide some form of encouragement primarily to youth of migrant backgrounds (and all youth for that matter) on the need to ensure mental health fitness in the first place, as much as possible.

LiME involves Fun Activities & Friendships

It is also meant to reassure them (including myself) that it is okay not to feel okay sometimes. It is more important though, to seek / call for help where applicable. Discussions around the topic of mental health and mental illness must be promoted as important, safe, and could be life-saving. We all have our own moments, episodes and even, periods of mental health challenges. It is only presented as different for different people, like many things of life. Let's talk about it!

7.1 Mental Health

According to the World Health Organization, mental health is "a state of well-being in which every individual realises his or her own potential, can cope with the normal stresses of life, can work productively and fruitfully, and is able to make a contribution to her or his community."

Mental health is sometimes used interchangeably with mental illness or mental health conditions such as depression, anxiety, personality disorder and other things. But the fact of the matter is that mental health isn't about the illnesses. It's about the well-being of a person.

To understand this a bit more, think of a continuum where mental health is at one end of the spectrum and is represented by feeling good and functioning well, while mental illness is at the other represented by symptoms that affect people's thoughts, feelings or behaviour. It is

> *Mental health is not just about mental illness. It is about your overall wellbeing. So let us talk more about it.*

important to be open to addressing mental illness, as doing this would move us closer to the good side of the mental health continuum.

7.2 Mental Illness

Mental illnesses are confusions of the brain functions. They have numerous causes and outcomes from tricky interactions between a person's genes and their environment.

Mental illnesses have been linked to biological factors as well as life experience like trauma or abuse, family history of mental health issues or abuse, clinical depression including feelings of sadness, uselessness, hopelessness or guilt. Also known to be associated with mental illnesses are sleeping problems, low energy, feeling numb or like nothing matters, loss of self-esteem, pulling away from people and usual activities and not enjoying things you once did. Other indicators of mental illnesses include experiencing severe mood swings, hearing voices or believing things that are not true, thinking of harming yourself or others and inability to perform daily tasks like taking care of children (for a parent) or getting to work or school.

We have learnt that some popular types of mental illnesses include bipolar disorder, schizophrenia, and anxiety.

7.3 Youth and Mental Illnesses

Your mental health, as a migrant youth, is very important. It is not something to be ashamed of even if you are on the mental illness area of the continuum. You should not put it aside and merely hope that things will sort out themselves. Indeed, young people are also prone to mental illnesses. There are other contributors or triggers to mental illnesses that youth need to be aware of, in addition to the causes presented in the section above. Issues relating to school stress like exams, bullying or peer pressure could lead to mental health problems if not picked up and addressed early.

> *If you see symptoms in your friends or anyone, try to help. Don't just stand on the sideline and think it is not your problem. Notify someone that can help.*

Finding short-term coping methods such as self-harm, taking drugs, alcohol and others doesn't help. It only makes the situation worse which could lead to suicide if not checked. Indeed, the large number of suicide deaths in young people aged 14-25 years is (and should) be a concern for all involved – young people, families, schools, government and the community at large.

As soon as thoughts of suicide start to form, go to someone you can trust and talk to them about it. Also, keep your parents in the loop. It may seem like they don't understand, but they do. They were once a teenager like you.

If you also see these symptoms in your friends or anyone, try to help them. Don't stand on the sideline and think it is not your problem. Notify a teacher, the school psychologist or a parent. You may need to treat it like emergency in some situations.

7.4 Achieving and Staying Mentally Healthy

Firstly, you need to ensure that you are mentally healthy on an ongoing basis. Prevention is better than cure. Seek information on how to keep mentally healthy and fit. Just like physical health and fitness, there are growing awareness of mental health exercise that you can do to ensure you remain healthy while keeping mental illness far away as much as possible.

Connect with supportive groups that will help you to be mentally healthy and not those that will pull you down into mental illness. Don't be afraid to try and reach out to people that can support your commitment to your own mental health. Of course, be nice to all your colleagues. But you should be firm in avoiding associations that are harmful to you short or long term. If you're new to a school, try finding the right groups and clubs of like minds. Ask trusted classmates, senior buddies and/or teachers for help in this regard.

Stay positive. This will be very hard especially when it feels like nothing is going right in your life. I suggest at the end of each day before you go to bed, think about what the positives are for the day. It might be little things such as you woke in the morning, you knew the answer to that question the teacher asked, your friend gave you their Netflix password, anything.

Get physically active. You can join your local basketball, football or soccer club. If you aren't into sports, there are local events happening in your area. Just check online or at your local council.

Try to help others. If you see that someone needs a helping hand, give it to them. It helps you feel good about yourself and it shows that you care.

Get enough sleep. 3 hours is not enough sleep. The recommended hours of sleep for a teenager is between 7 - 8 hours. If you have a test or assessment the next day and you feel like staying up to study is the best option, it isn't. I know that procrastination will definitely lead to this, but it is a lesson for when you have another assessment in the future.

> *We can apply the SMART principles to mental health as well*

Set goals. This gives you something to look forward to and it builds a healthy habit. It is also beneficial for you because you have a record of how much you have grown as a person. I suggest using the SMART goal template:

S - set a specific goal

M - Is the goal measurable (can you keep track of that goal)?

A - Is the goal achievable (can you achieve the goal)?

R - Is your goal realistic?

T - Is your goal time-bound (can your goal be achieved in a certain timeframe)?

Communication is key. Trying to handle this on your own is not going to work. Your parents and friends aren't mind readers. You need to communicate to them what is happening to you.

If you are already experiencing symptoms of mental illness, do not feel too bad; you are not alone. Many young people are becoming more aware and accepting of mental illnesses as real as other diseases such as liver disease or cancer. It is not a weakness nor is it necessarily a character flaw. Get help and do this early, not later. Start with talking to a trusted friend, a teacher or a family member. You may also need to get timely professional help. Organisations such as Beyond Blue, MindSpot Clinic, headspace, Lifeline, Black Dog Institute, Relationship Australia and SANE Australia provide information on how to deal with mental illnesses and ensuring better outcomes.

Achieving and staying mentally healthy should be your goal. Strive to keep a positive outlook on life irrespective of your past and current situations in life. This will allow you to realize your full potential, cope with the stresses of life, work productively and make meaningful contributions to your family, peers and communities.

References:

- Beyond Blue (www.beyondblue.org.au): What is mental health? Assessed 27 May 2019

- Australian Government's Department of Health (www.health.gov.au): What is mental illness? Assessed 27 May 2019
- TeenMentalHealth.org (n.d.): Mental Disorders. Assessed 27 May 2019

> *Please take further action/s I you Mink you need help with your mental health after reading this Chapter or any other part of this book. In Australia, you can call Lifeline on 13 11 14 or Beyond Blue on 1300 224 636 where mental illness or related concerns may be involved and deserves emergency action. Do not hesitate to call 000 for emergency police and/orambulance, if necessary. Readers in other counties should call equivalent emergency contacts in their countries, as applicable.*

Reflection 7.0:

- How much do you know about your mental health and wellness? Take some time to write down a few thoughts about what you knew before reading this chapter and after. Do you think there's a need to know more awareness for yourself and peers?

  _____

  _____

  _____

- How easy is it to openly discuss the topic of mental health and mental illness amongst your friends, in your family, and in your community? How do you think this situation can be improved in view of the urgency for intervention, sometimes?

  _____

  _____

  _____

- What actions will you undertake to achieve (where applicable) and stay mentally healthy? How will you contribute to the solution of making it easier for young people to be more open about their mental health status? Write down some answers which will help you to stay on track with this important topic.

  _____

  _____

  _____

8.0 Concluding Remarks

LiME Youth

We are LiMErs – leaders in motion and experience. Obviously, we still have a lot to learn along our pathways of life in general and as people of migrant backgrounds. Some of us were born here in Australia. Others were born overseas and came over and settled here. We all now live in this blessed country where most things work very well most of the time. The opportunities for young people are diverse and numerous. The education, employment and business opportunities, technological advancement, entertainment and welfare system are about the best globally. We will continue to position ourselves in order to maximise our benefits of being a youth in this prosperous nation.

We also see, experience and hear the challenges confronting youth, today, and most likely, into the future. These have been highlighted in this book starting with the context of those of migrant backgrounds in Australia, with applicable principles to all youth in the country and beyond.

Despite the advantages of multiculturalism, it is being threatened as evidenced in cases of stereotyping, racism and discrimination. The successes of LiME and similar programs have further affirmed that the younger generation present a viable hope for multiculturalism.

A Handbook for Migrant Youth

LiMErs: Catalysts for Positive Influence

Concluding Remarks

The negative impacts of unrestrained indulgence in social media and gaming is another challenge highlighted as an outcome of LiME Think Tank and expressed in this book. It is important to "strike the right balance". The youth in the midst of the situation must take primary responsibility for this balance and positively embrace the challenge of maintaining their healthy online presence. However, all stakeholders must provide a helping hand. Migrants Professional Bridge Incorporated (MPB) has made a significant contribution via the LiME initiative. More can, and should, be done.

One final challenge highlighted in this book is mental health / illness especially with regards to the associated stigma, secrecy and trauma (including deaths, sorrow and losses). LiME Youth have added their voices to the ongoing wellness campaign. *It's okay not to be okay sometimes*, it's okay to ask a mate "are you okay?" as often as it is necessary. It is okay to take measures to ensure mental health fitness in the first instance, and it is also okay to seek and enjoy treatment for mental illness, where applicable.

LiME provided us with opportunities for self-discovery, to be challenged, to be mentored, while developing our communication, leadership, project, financial, entrepreneurial and team skills. We also developed valuable friendships. This book is a token of the lessons we have learnt along the way. However, this is not the end, but rather, the beginning, as we continue to develop and celebrate our youth, our multiculturalism and our contributions to the good of mankind and society.

You may also be interested in the following books by Ephraim Osaghae, LiME Project Leader and Founder of Migrants Professional Bridge Incorporated (MPB).

A Handbook for Migrants: The Good, The Challenges and The Lessons
A Reflective Guide for Meaningful and Whole-Life Experience

Migrants are important contributors to the success and growth of many countries. But they face series of challenges before they can fully attain whole-life balance while integrating into their new countries. These challenges are real, and to some, they have become sources of worry and despair.

As such, each migrant needs all the help that he or she can get. This book provides that, and much more. It is a reflective guide about the beneficial aspects of migration, the social, economic and cultural challenges, as well as associated solutions. All these are presented from a migrant's point of view, and with anecdotes from someone that has walked the path — someone who is keen to share lessons learned so that it will be more comfortable and more rewarding for others, especially those coming behind.

In this book, you will find the following:

- Who really is a migrant?
- The career and business challenges of a migrant; and proposed solutions.
- The challenges and lessons with regards to family life including raising children and youths.
- The essential aspects and preparation for aging and retirement.
- The importance of communities and leadership.
- The lived experiences of a migrant.

You will find great use for the content of this book if you are:

- Intending migrants looking for pre-migration considerations and tips.
- Migrants looking for guidance in work, families, youths and community engagements.
- Non-migrants, students, policymakers, service providers and community leaders.

This book also allows you to participate in meaningful conversations on migrant experiences.

VOICES FROM *Home*

A NARRATION OF PARENTS OF FIRST-GENERATION MIGRANTS

WISDOM FROM OUR DIASPORIC ROOTS

EPHRAIM OSAGHAE MBL

Voices from Home: Wisdom from Our Diasporic Roots A Narration of Parents of First Generation Migrants

- This book informs global audiences about some key aspects of lived experiences of people of migrant backgrounds starting with the Australian context.
- It contributes to the value-adding conversations around the themes of identity, sustainable migration, diasporic roots, extended families, cross-cultural intelligence, integration, and other socio-economic aspects of migration.
- It provides insights on the key dynamics and interplay of cultures, underpinning motivations, and extended family structures of typical 1st gen migrants.
- It provides hints and tips for new, emerging and established migrants on how to support family members back in their countries of birth.
- It should inspire people of migrant backgrounds to revisit their family trees, write their stories and celebrate their roots. The value will include documented accounts of their heritage and benefits to immediate families and generations to come.
- This book will provide hints and tips for policy making, alignment and implementation especially in the areas of sustainable migration.
- It is a resource material for intending migrants as they prepare for their migration journeys, as well as new and emerging migrants, especially with lessons learnt on how to position

Concluding Remarks

themselves and families for more meaningful migration experiences.
- Finally, this book serves as a legacy to Jacob & Grace, the narrators of the primary content of this book. They are much loved. To their health, peace and fulfillment...

LiME is an initiative of Migrants Professional Bridge Incorporated (MPB) which is also known as Aus-Professional-Bridge (APB).

MPB advances and supports the empowerment, capacity building, and vocational integration of skilled and semi-skilled people of migrant backgrounds enabling them to sustainably participate in socio-economic wellbeing and growth for themselves, their families and Australia.

Some MPB activities include the following:

- Providing networking opportunities and ongoing employment support services to people of migrant backgrounds enabling them to acquire the required local networks and strategies to secure and hold jobs.
- Providing counselling, coaching and mentoring services and support to bridge the gaps caused by lack of suitable capabilities, culture shocks, displacement from career paths, and other such challenges.
- Providing training for up-skilling and/or right-skilling to ensure suitable competencies and qualifications.
- Providing work experience and employment including volunteering opportunities.
- Providing a vehicle for more experienced professionals, philanthropic individuals, groups and organisations to contribute to the cause.
- Facilitating professional integration including career buddy, where applicable.

Concluding Remarks

- Facilitating professionally-aligned programs to engage and empower youths in these disadvantaged communities - "guide them young." LiME is an example of this passion.
- Providing, education / referral, advisory, advocacy, and representation services to people of migrant backgrounds in their bid for a fair go for opportunities and sustainability for their chosen professions.

MPB's Slogan: Facilitating diversity, inclusion & participation . . . providing opportunities for people, businesses and communities.

Use the following contact details to learn more and/or enquire about LiME MPB:

Email: admin@mpbgroup.org.au
Website: www.mpbgroup.org.au

You can also connect via:

- LinkedIn (search with Migrants' Professional Bridge (MPB) Incorporated),
- Twitter (@mpbgroup),
- Facebook (@mpbgroup1), and
- Instagram (@mpbgroup)

www.ingramcontent.com/pod-product-compliance
Lightning Source LLC
Chambersburg PA
CBHW070309010526
44107CB00056B/2542